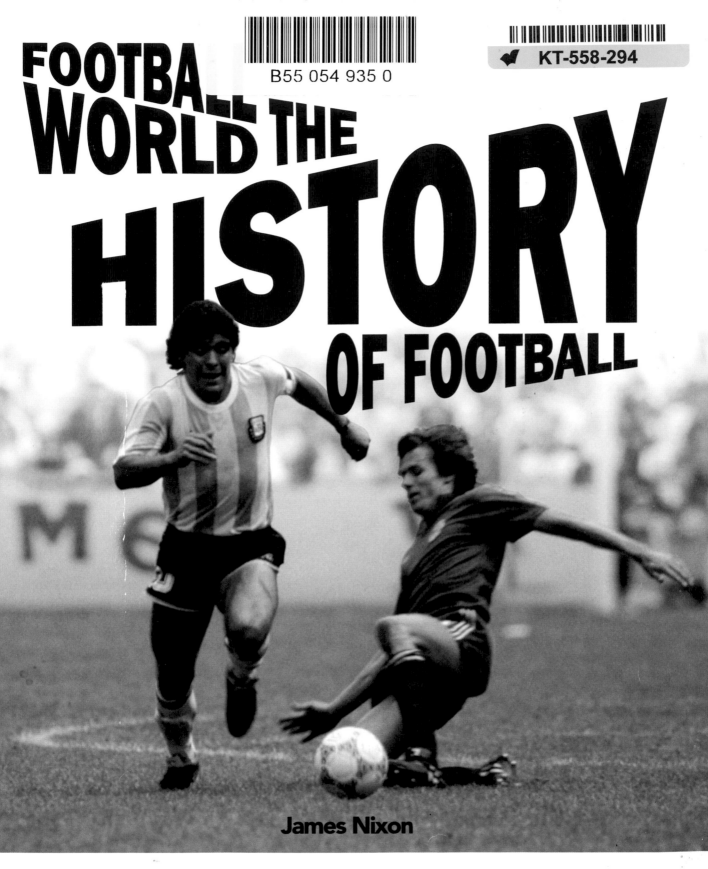

FOOTBALL WORLD

THE HISTORY OF FOOTBALL

James Nixon

FRANKLIN WATTS
LONDON·SYDNEY

Franklin Watts
First published in Great Britain in 2017 by The Watts Publishing Group

Credits
Editor: James Nixon
Design: Keith Williams, sprout.uk.com
Planning and production by Discovery Books Limited

Photo credits: Cover image: Getty Images (Jean-Yves Ruszniewski).
Getty Images: pp. 5 (Popperfoto), 6 (Popperfoto), 10 (Bob Thomas/Popperfoto), 13 top (Keystone/
Stringer), 14 (Art Rickerby/The LIFE Picture Collection), 15 top (Popperfoto), 17 bottom (Central Press/
Stringer), 18 (Popperfoto), 20 (STF/AFP), 21 top, 21 bottom (Bob Thomas), 22 (Jean-Yves Ruszniewski), 24
(Bob Thomas), 27 (Ben Radford).
Shutterstock: pp. 8 (Herbert Kratky), 9 top (David Spieth), 13 bottom (Yury Dmitrienko), 17 top
(ATGImages), 23 (Diego Silvestre), 26 (Eoghan McNally), 28 top and bottom (katatonia82), 29 top (Christian
Bertrand), 29 bottom (Marco Iacobucci EPP).
Wikimedia: pp. 4, 7 (FIFA Museum Collection), 9 bottom (Smabs Sputzer), 11 (Oldelpaso), 12
(FOTO:Fortepan), 15 bottom, 16 (Dutch National Archives), 19 top (Nicki Dugan Pogue), 19 bottom
(CeeGee).

ISBN: 978 1 4451 5562 3

Printed in Dubai

Franklin Watts
An imprint of
Hachette Children's Group
Part of The Watts Publishing Group
Carmelite House
50 Victoria Embankment
London EC4Y 0DZ

An Hachette UK Company
www.hachette.co.uk

www.franklinwatts.co.uk

The statistics in this book were correct at the time of printing, but because
of the nature of sport, it cannot be guaranteed that they are now accurate.

Every effort has been made by the Publishers to ensure that the websites
in this book are suitable for children, that they are of the highest
educational value, and that they contain no inappropriate or offensive
material. However, because of the nature of the Internet, it is impossible
to guarantee that the contents of these sites will not be altered. We
strongly advise that Internet access is supervised by a responsible adult.

CONTENTS

IN THE BEGINNING

Today, the game of football is played across the world by millions. So where did it all start? Football officially started in England in 1863, but people enjoyed kicking a ball about for centuries before that.

Ancient games

As far back as the third century BCE, a similar game called 'cuju' was played in China. It involved kicking a ball stuffed with feathers and hairs through a small opening into a net. The net was fixed onto long bamboo canes. Cuju matches were often held inside the emperor's palace.

The ancient Greeks played a ball game called *episkyros*. Two teams of around 12 to 14 players attempted to kick or throw the ball over a white line behind their opponents. *Harpastum* was a similar game played by the ancient Romans, but with a much smaller ball.

Mob football

The origins of modern football lie in the chaotic kick-abouts that took place in **medieval** Britain. Known as 'mob football', matches were often bruising contests between towns or villages with an unlimited number of players. There was little in the way of rules and certainly no referees. The mass of people did whatever they could to move the ball towards their target. The ball was often made out of an inflated pig's bladder!

An ancient Greek footballer balances the ball on his thigh.

FLASH FACT

Mob football matches between villages would take place through streets, across fields and over streams. Sometimes the target was to kick the ball into the opposing team's church!

Making rules

A turning point for the game came in the early nineteenth century. Football had become popular in England's famous **public schools**, which were no place for the hurly-burly of mob football. As football became part of the school curriculum, the sport became more organised. Schools such as Harrow and Eton developed a game that encouraged skilful dribbling. Other schools, such as Cheltenham and Rugby, preferred a more rugged game where hands could be used.

In 1848, Cambridge University attempted to draw up the first set of common rules. The Cambridge Rules allowed **goal kicks** and throw-ins, but prevented running while holding the ball. However, schools continued to play their own versions of football.

Sheffield Football Club played a key role in the development of modern football with the rules they laid down in 1857. It introduced the idea of corners and **free kicks** for **fouls**.

THE BIRTH OF THE FA

On 26 October 1863, 11 London football clubs met up to finally agree on a set of common rules. At this meeting, the Football Association (FA) was formed, the first of its kind. The day marked the start of modern football.

Splitting with rugby

The FA had to quickly sort out the confusion of different rules and regulations. Most clubs were unhappy with rules that allowed carrying the ball, shin-kicking and tripping. So after six meetings, supporters of a rugby-style game walked out on the FA and organised their own sport (rugby football union). The FA could now create the 'Laws of the Game' without further argument. In December 1863, the first match under the new rules was played between London sides Barnes and Richmond.

Growing the game

Within eight years of its formation, the FA already had 50 member clubs. The FA's secretary Charles Alcock believed it was time to set up a national **knockout** tournament. And so the FA Cup was born, the oldest football competition in the world. Wanderers beat Royal Engineers 1-0 in the first final in 1872, watched by 2,000 spectators.

England played Scotland at the Oval cricket ground in London in 1875.

Stat Tracker

First 12 league clubs (1889)	Titles won since 1889
Preston North End	2
Aston Villa	7
Wolverhampton Wanderers	3
Blackburn Rovers	3
Bolton Wanderers	0
West Bromwich Albion	1
Accrington (folded 1896)	0
Everton	9
Burnley	2
Derby County	2
Notts County	0
Stoke City	0

The first international

In 1870, Charles Alcock had another bright idea. He thought England should take on Scotland. After a few experimental games, the first official **international** took place in November 1872 at the West of Scotland Cricket Club. The Scots wore dark blue shirts and the English wore white shirts, just like they do today. The 0-0 draw was contested in front of a crowd of 4,000 people. The Scottish FA was formed in 1873, followed by the Welsh FA in 1875.

FLASH FACT

*The teams' **formations** in the first England-Scotland international looked like a very attacking style on paper. Scotland played a 2-2-6 formation while England played a 1-1-8 with eight strikers!*

Going pro

Clubs soon wanted to pay their players for doing their job. The FA made this legal in 1885. Players could now become professionals. Next, the top clubs needed regular fixtures organised. This led to the creation of the Football League, which was first contested by 12 teams. In 1889, Preston North End topped the table to become the first ever English league champions.

A team picture of the first Football League winners, Preston North End.

THE LAWS OF THE GAME

Modern football may have begun in 1863, but the game was very different back then. Gradually the rules have changed to help turn football into the most popular sport on the planet.

The original rulebook

The rulebook created in 1863 still contained laws that today seem more at home on the rugby field. Players were allowed to throw the ball to a teammate if they made a 'fair catch'. If a player touched the ball beyond the opponent's goal line they gained the chance of a free kick at goal. Goals could be scored at any height because there was no crossbar. The old **offside** law meant that no forward passes of any kind were allowed. And there was no rule to say that the ball had to be round!

Major changes

The first big rule changes were made in 1866. The 'fair catch' was eliminated. Forward passes became legal as long as there were three opponents between the receiver and the goal. This was the first move towards the modern offside law and transformed the game from a mass of dribbling to a game filled with passing. By 1871 tape was added to make a crossbar between the two goalposts and the position of goalkeeper was introduced.

Red cards were introduced in 1970, more than a hundred years after the birth of football.

The lines on the pitch, such as the penalty box, were gradually added over time.

Football firsts

Goal kicks first became part of the rules in 1869 and corner kicks followed in 1872. A crossbar replaced tape in 1875. There was no such thing as a **penalty** until 1891. Back then it was called the 'kick of death' and could be taken anywhere along a 11-metre line. The first time referees were given the power to give free kicks for fouls and send players off was in 1891. In 1902, it was decided to create a penalty box and penalty spot.

Subs, cards and back passes

In 1965, English Football League clubs were allowed to make **substitutes** for the first time. It wasn't until 1995 that teams could make three substitutes. The use of yellow and red cards began at the 1970 World Cup in Mexico.

Football rules are still tinkered with. In 1992, a new rule meant goalkeepers were forbidden from picking up a back pass from a teammate – this prevented defenders from timewasting. In 2017, video assistant referees (VARs) were first used – they look at video replays and help the referee to make the right decisions.

TALES FROM HISTORY

In the 1956 FA Cup final, Manchester City goalkeeper Bert Trautmann collided heavily with a Birmingham City attacker. Trautmann felt dazed and wobbly and his neck looked crooked, but no substitutes were allowed, so he carried on. With some heroic, crucial saves, Trautmann guided his team to victory. After the match, doctors discovered that Trautmann had in fact played on with a broken neck!

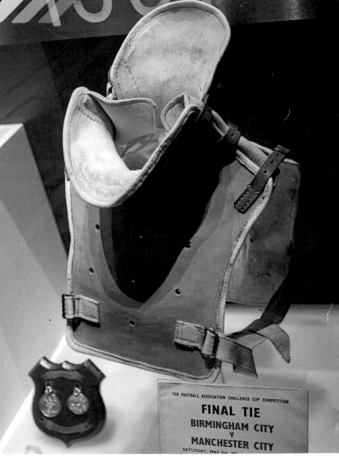

After his life-threatening injury, Bert Trautmann missed most of the next season and had to wear this neck brace.

THE WORLD GAME

From its origins in Britain, football rapidly reached all parts of the world. By 1893 football associations had been formed as far away as New Zealand and Argentina. It was clear that a global organisation was needed.

Forming FIFA

FIFA was founded in 1904 by seven European countries to oversee the worldwide game. By 1912, 21 nations had joined FIFA, including countries outside Europe such as Chile and South Africa. A year later the United States and Canada also entered. In the 1920s, FIFA started organising Olympic Games' football tournaments and began plans for its own world championship.

Uruguay thrashed hosts France 5-1 at the 1924 Olympics.

First competitions

The popularity of football grew fast in South America. In 1916, teams on the continent took part in the first version of a tournament now known as the Copa América – the oldest international continental football competition.

At the 1924 Olympics, South American side Uruguay joined the United States, Egypt and 19 European teams in what would be the largest international tournament until the 1982 World Cup. It was the first time a team from South America had faced a team from Europe in a football competition.

Uruguay, who had won the first two Copa América titles, triumphed 3-0 over Switzerland in the final. A crowd of 60,000 spectators watched, fascinated to see how the South Americans played football. Uruguay were gold-medal winners again four years later.

FLASH FACT

In the 1930 World Cup final, Argentina and Uruguay argued over which ball to use. So Argentina's ball was used for the first half and Uruguay's in the second half!

The balls used in the 1930 World Cup final are now on display at the National Football Museum in Preston, England. Argentina's is shown on the left and Uruguay's on the right.

The World Cup

In 1928, FIFA announced that Uruguay was to **host** the first FIFA World Cup in 1930. For European teams this was going to mean an expensive trip by ship across the Atlantic Ocean. FIFA eventually persuaded France, Belgium, Romania and **Yugoslavia** to make the trip. Of the 13 teams that took part, Uruguay were victorious yet again, beating Argentina 4-2 in the final. The tournament captivated the public – 93,000 attended the final with thousands more shut outside the stadium.

Italy on top

The difficulty of travel continued at early World Cups. Brazil were the only South American team willing to travel to the 1934 and 1938 tournaments held in Europe. Italy won both tournaments and remain the only team to have won two World Cups under the same manager – Vittorio Pozzo. In France in 1938, Italy also became the first team to win a World Cup on foreign soil.

EUROPEAN CHALLENGE

In 1954, the Union of European Football Associations (UEFA) was formed and there were soon big European tournaments for both clubs and countries. It soon became apparent that England, the inventors of football, actually had a lot to learn from their European rivals.

TALES FROM HISTORY

Hungary were hot favourites to win the 1954 World Cup in Switzerland. In the final they met **West Germany** who they had already thrashed 8-3 in the group stage. When Hungary took a 2-0 lead inside the first ten minutes, the result looked inevitable. However, the rain lashed down and the Germans were wearing newly designed boots suited to the conditions. The underdogs roared back to an unlikely 3-2 win. The game is remembered as the 'Miracle of Bern'.

Magical Magyars

The Hungary national football team in the early 1950s were so good that they were known as the Magical **Magyars**. In 1953, as the world-ranked number-one team, they beat England 6-3 in a game dubbed the 'Match of the Century'. Hungary had 35 shots on goal – England had just five.

The Magical Magyars were supremely fit, highly skilled and outwitted teams with their clever tactics. England travelled to Hungary for a rematch in 1954 and were destroyed 7-1. This remains England's biggest ever defeat!

Hungarian Ferenc Puskás (above) was a magical striker. He scored 84 international goals in 85 games!

Alfredo Di Stefano (right) scores the first of Real Madrid's seven goals in the 1960 European Cup final.

European cups

In 1955, UEFA created the European Cup for the best clubs in Europe, now known as the Champions League. Spanish side Real Madrid completely dominated the early years. They won the first five European Cups in a row, inspired by their superstar strikers Ferenc Puskás and Italian Alfredo Di Stefano. In the 1960 final, Madrid destroyed German team Eintracht Frankfurt 7-3. Puskás scored four and Di Stefano netted the other three!

The original European Cup trophy was given to Real Madrid for their achievements and replaced with this one in 1967.

UEFA started running a Cup Winner's Cup in 1960. It was a tournament for every nation's cup winners around Europe, such as the FA Cup winners. The first competition was won by Italian club Fiorentina who defeated Scotland's Rangers 4-1 over two **legs**.

The European Championships (Euros) also began in 1960. The tournament would crown one nation as champion of Europe every four years. Up until 1980, just four teams qualified for the final tournament. The **Soviet Union** triumphed in 1960, winning a tense match 2-1 against Yugoslavia in **extra time**.

FLASH FACT

The Ballon d'Or (European Footballer of the Year) has been awarded since 1956. The first winner was 41-year-old Blackpool and England winger Stanley Matthews, otherwise known as 'The Wizard of the Dribble'.

BRAZIL'S GOLDEN ERA

Between 1958 and 1970 Brazil were undoubtedly the greatest team on the planet. In that time, Brazil won three World Cups. It is often said of football, 'The English invented it, the Brazilians perfected it.'

Enter Pelé

In 1958, a 17-year-old named Pelé arrived at the World Cup largely unknown. This was about to change. In the quarter-final 1-0 win over Wales, Pelé became the youngest World Cup scorer ever. He followed this with a **hat-trick** against France in the semi-final. In the final Pelé outshone everyone, scoring two more goals as Brazil thumped hosts Sweden 5-2.

Pelé (right) is the only player to have won three World Cups (1958, 1962 and 1970).

TALES FROM HISTORY

Brazil's 1958 victory made up for the disappointment they had suffered eight years earlier. Brazil were the 1950 World Cup hosts and expected to win. On the day of the final, a carnival was organised to celebrate the title. Over 200,000 people packed into the stadium to watch the game. But Uruguay stunned the stadium into silence with a 2-1 victory. The pain of defeat was so great that Brazil changed the colour of their kit from white to the yellow that they still wear today!

Garrincha (left) scored twice to help Brazil beat England 3-1 in the 1962 World quarter-finals.

The best team ever

It was at the 1970 World Cup that many people think Brazil perfected football. Brazil fielded an awesome squad that played some of the most beautiful, attacking football ever seen. In 1970, Pelé was brilliant, scoring four times in his final World Cup. The powerful Jairzinho, nicknamed 'The Hurricane', scored in every single game and seven in total.

In the final, Brazil taught Italy a footballing lesson, thrashing them 4-1. The final goal was one of the greatest World Cup goals ever. Eight different Brazilian players touched the ball in a superb passing move that ended with captain Carlos Alberto steaming up the right wing and smashing the ball into the net.

World stars

Pelé became a national hero and a star around the whole world. Quick, powerful, with electrifying skill, and known for spectacular goals, Pelé was voted World Player of the Century in 1999.

At the 1962 World Cup it was a different Brazilian who made the headlines. With Pelé injured early on in the tournament, it was the winger Garrincha who led Brazil to glory. Garrincha was an extraordinary dribbler and shooter. His legs were bent strangely, which seemed to help him burst past defenders at unusual angles. Garrincha scored twice in both the quarter- and semi-finals and was named the Player of the Tournament.

FLASH FACT

For winning a third World Cup in 1970, Brazil was given the Jules Rimet Trophy (right) to keep permanently. A new trophy was designed for future tournaments.

BRITISH GLORY

The 1960s were a golden age for British football. Clubs and country tasted success for the first time in major tournaments.

Super Spurs

Tottenham Hotspur crushed Atlético Madrid 5-1 in the 1963 Cup Winners' Cup final. They became the first British team to win a European trophy. Goal machine Jimmy Greaves scored two of Spurs' goals.

1966 World Cup

West Ham United won the Cup Winners' Cup in 1965. Three members of the team would go on and play a major part in England's 1966 World Cup final victory – the goalscorers Geoff Hurst and Martin Peters, and legendary captain Bobby Moore.

World Cup hosts England reached the final with a 2-1 win over Portugal, thanks to goals from 1966 European Footballer of the Year Bobby Charlton. Jimmy Greaves was back from injury and fit to play in the final. However, manager Alf Ramsay decided to stick with his back-up striker Geoff Hurst. It proved to be a masterstroke. Hurst led England to a 4-2 victory over West Germany, scoring the only hat-trick to ever be scored in a World Cup final.

FLASH FACT

*Jimmy Greaves has scored more goals (357) in the history of the English **top flight** than anyone else. Greaves has also scored the most hat-tricks for England (6).*

West Ham and England captain Bobby Moore (in white) was one of the best defenders and tacklers of his era.

Champions of Europe

In 1967, British football triumphed again. Scottish side Celtic became the first British club to be crowned champions of Europe. Manager Jock Stein was the mastermind behind the 2-1 final win over Italians Inter Milan. Inter had taken an early lead and were famous for their defensive tactics. But Celtic's inventive, attacking football was rewarded with a winning goal from Stevie Chalmers with six minutes left.

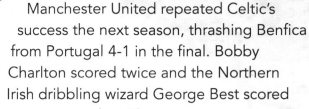

JOHN "JOCK" STEIN CBE

5th October 1922

10th September 1985

Manchester United repeated Celtic's success the next season, thrashing Benfica from Portugal 4-1 in the final. Bobby Charlton scored twice and the Northern Irish dribbling wizard George Best scored another. The victory came just ten years after the team were involved in a plane crash in Munich, Germany, where it lost eight of its young, bright stars. Manager Matt Busby was also left close to death but survived to guide his team to glory.

Hurst (bottom right) scores England's third goal in the 1966 World Cup final, but did it really cross the line?

TALES FROM HISTORY

Geoff Hurst's crucial third goal for England in the 1966 World Cup final was one of the most controversial moments in football history. The score was 2-2 in extra time when Hurst's shot bounced down off the crossbar onto the goal line. The TV cameras did not show if it was a goal; the referee wasn't sure either, but the goal was given.

In the last moments of the game West Germany streamed forward but were counter-attacked. When Hurst scored again, the commentator's famous words were: 'Some people are on the pitch, they think its all over – it is now!'

WOMEN'S FOOTBALL

Today, football is played by more women than any other team sport on the globe. Yet in Britain, women's football took a long time to develop because the FA banned it for nearly 50 years.

Early days

The first women's match on record took place in Glasgow in 1892. It wasn't long before the women's game became hugely popular. During the First World War, women who worked in the factories supplying **munitions** formed their own football clubs. Playing football was good for wartime morale. In 1917, a tournament was launched in the north-east of England for munitions workers called the Munitionettes Cup.

Dick, Kerr's Ladies were undefeated British champions in the 1920-1921 season.

Crowd pleasers

Dick, Kerr's Ladies, formed from a wartime factory in 1917, were one of the best teams of the era. They played their matches at Preston North End's ground Deepdale and drew massive crowds. In a game against St Helen's Ladies played at Everton's Goodison Park, 53,000 spectators came to watch. Dick, Kerr's Ladies raised thousands of pounds for wartime charities. In 1920, the team played the first women's international against France in front of 25,000 people and won 2-0.

USA celebrate winning a third World Cup in 2015.

The ban

By 1921 there were around 150 women's teams in England. Then the FA decided to ban women's matches from all FA grounds, claiming that the game was unsuitable for women. The chance to play in front of big crowds was over, and the ban set women's football back by decades.

Revival

Three years after the buzz and excitement of the 1966 World Cup, an English Women's FA was formed. Two years later, in 1971, the FA finally lifted its ban on women's football matches being played at FA grounds. Since the 1980s, a host of major competitions have been launched at international and national levels. The European Women's Championship (Women's Euros) began in 1984, where an England team were beaten on penalties in the final by Sweden.

Growing the game

Japan's L-League was set up in 1989 and became one of the first professional leagues for women in the world. Top internationals from Europe, America and Asia went to play in Japan as it was the only place to make a living.

The first Women's World Cup was held in China in 1991. The United States defeated Norway 2-1 in the final and have been the most successful nation in world tournaments since, winning four World Cups and four Olympic titles. Despite receiving less TV coverage, women's football continues to grow in popularity.

FLASH FACT

Germany have dominated the Women's Euros. Between 1995 and 2013 they won the tournament six times in a row!

Germany (in white) play Turkey in a Euro 2017 qualifying match.

TOTAL FOOTBALL

In the 1970s, the Dutch invented a majestic style of football. It came to be known as 'total football' and helped the Netherlands reach two World Cup finals.

The mastermind

Rinus Michels, the manager of Ajax Amsterdam, was the mastermind behind total football. In his system, players continually switched positions as the game was played. Every player needed to be skilful on the ball, fast and fit. It was a very attacking style and a joy to watch.

Using a 'total football' system, Ajax played some of the finest football ever seen. The Dutch side won the European Cup three times in a row between 1971 and 1973.

The two Johans

Ajax's Johan Cruyff was one of the greatest footballers to have played the game. Total football suited Cruyff, who was full of tricks and pace. He could wander all over the pitch and find the space where he could do the most damage. Cruyff's transfer to Barcelona in 1973 for a world record fee signalled the end of Ajax's dominance.

Johan Neeskens helped Cruyff to shine. Neeskens was a central midfielder who did so much running it was like his side had an extra player on the pitch. He was tough as well as being highly skilled. Neeskens followed Cruyff to Barcelona in 1974.

Cruyff dribbles around the goalkeeper in a 4-0 demolition of Argentina in the 1974 World Cup quarter-final.

World Cup heartache

Rinus Michels was hired as the Netherlands manager for the 1974 World Cup. The stage was set for total football to become famous. The Netherlands were easily the best team of the tournament. Cruyff and Neeskens each scored in a 2-1 victory over Brazil to send the Dutch to the final. In the final, Neeskens scored a penalty for the Netherlands before West Germany had even touched the ball. But the Germans turned it round to win 2-1 and break Dutch hearts.

In 1978, the Netherlands were runners-up again. This time it was hosts Argentina who were victorious. Like the Magical Magyars of the 1950s, the Dutch side were a great team that never won football's greatest prize.

Golden Boot winner Mario Kempes scored his second goal in extra time to help Argentina win the 1978 World Cup final 3-1.

Marco Van Basten's super volley helped the Netherlands win their first major trophy at the 1988 European Championships.

TALES FROM HISTORY

Rinus Michels made a triumphant return when he managed the Netherlands to European Championship glory in 1988. Victory in the semi-final over hosts West Germany was sweet, as the Dutch finally got their revenge for 1974. The Netherlands' 2-0 win in the final against the Soviet Union is famous for one of the most spectacular goals in football history. With the ball falling from high out of the sky, Marco Van Basten blistered a **volley** from a ridiculously sharp angle over the goalkeeper and into the net.

TRIUMPH AND TRAGEDY

Michel Platini lifts the trophy for France at Euro 1984.

The 1980s was marked by some astonishing individual performances, but also by some of the worst tragedies in the history of football.

Italy reign again

In 1982, Italy won their first World Cup for 44 years. Striker Paulo Rossi was their leading man. Rossi scored a hat-trick in a thrilling game to knock out favourites Brazil. He scored two more goals in the semi-final and opened the scoring in a 3-1 win over West Germany in the final.

FLASH FACT

Paulo Rossi is the most recent person to win a World Cup, the Golden Boot and the **Golden Ball** award at the same tournament. Garrincha in 1962 and Mario Kempes in 1978 achieved the same feat.

The king

The top footballer in the early 1980s was French midfielder Michel Platini. Platini was one of the best passers in football history and a **prolific** goalscorer. It earned him the nickname 'The King'. While he played for Italian giants Juventus, Platini was awarded the Ballon d'Or three times in a row between 1983 and 1985.

Platini put in an incredible performance to help France win the 1984 European Championships on home soil. As captain, Platini scored nine goals in France's five matches, including two hat-tricks!

God's gift

Some say that Diego Maradona from Argentina was the most naturally gifted footballer the world has ever seen. Maradona stood at just 1.65 metres tall, but had mesmerising dribbling skills and ball control.

At the 1986 World Cup, Maradona put on his greatest show. Maradona captained Argentina to a 3-2 final victory over West Germany. Having scored or set up ten of Argentina's 14 goals in the tournament, Maradona was awarded the Golden Ball.

Disasters

Victory for Michel Platini's Juventus in the 1985 European Cup final was ruined by tragedy. When Liverpool supporters charged at Juventus fans, 39 people were killed when they were crushed against a wall that eventually collapsed. UEFA banned English clubs from European competitions for five years.

Worse was to follow in 1989. Ninety-six Liverpool fans were killed when they were crushed to death during an FA Cup semi-final at Hillsborough Stadium in Sheffield. The disasters in the 1980s led to changes that made stadiums and football matches much safer.

Diego Maradona was an incredible player who was worshipped by his fans.

TALES FROM HISTORY

Argentina's 2-1 win over England in the 1986 World Cup quarter final showed the two sides of Maradona – the genius, and the villain. Maradona gave Argentina the lead by jumping above the English goalkeeper and punching the ball into the net! Maradona celebrated like he had done nothing wrong. The goal became known as 'The Hand of God'.

Just four minutes later, Maradona scored what is now called 'Goal of the Century'. From his own half, Maradona dribbled past five players and more than half the length of the field before slotting the ball past England's keeper.

A NEW DAWN

Football was given a makeover in the 1990s. New competitions were created and innovations changed the way tournaments were played.

Premier League

In 1992, clubs in England's First Division separated from the rest of the Football League to form their own top-flight. They called it the Premier League and TV stations paid big money to screen it. The Premier League was then able to attract skilful players from all over the world.

Champions League

The UEFA Champions League replaced the European Cup in 1992. The trophy was kept the same, but the tournament now included a group stage. Each group was like a mini-league and contained four teams. It was no longer a straight knockout competition.

Into America

The United States embraced football (or soccer as the Americans call it) in the 1990s. The women's national side had already won the first women's World Cup in 1991 when the US hosted the men's World Cup in 1994. The average attendance for games at the tournament was a whopping 68,991. This was a World Cup record that still stands today. Brazil beat Italy in the first World Cup final to be decided on a **penalty shoot-out**.

After the 1994 World Cup, the US launched Major League Soccer (MLS), a championship for North American clubs.

Germany celebrate Oliver Bierhoff's winning golden goal in the Euro 96 final.

Expansions

More nations had the chance to qualify and experience the thrills of major tournaments in the late '90s. The 1996 Euros, held in England, doubled the size of the competition from eight to 16 teams. The 1998 World Cup in France increased the number of teams from 24 to 32.

Golden goal

A rule called the 'golden goal' was introduced at Euro 96. The idea was to avoid matches ending in penalties. If a team scored during extra time they won the match immediately. Euro 96 was decided by a golden goal when Germany scored five minutes into extra time against the Czech Republic. However, extra time often became boring, as sides were too scared to concede a goal and lose the match. FIFA abandoned golden goals after Euro 2004.

TALES FROM HISTORY

At both the World Cup in 1990 and Euro 96, England suffered agonising semi-final defeat in a penalty shoot-out. And both times it was against Germany, who would go on to become champions. English players that missed their spot kicks became famous for the wrong reason. England defender Gareth Southgate was the villain at Euro 96, hitting his vital penalty straight at the keeper. Germany scored their next penalty and were through to the final, whilst England were out.

THE RISE OF FRANCE

France were top dogs in international football by the end of the twentieth century and won their first ever World Cup at the 1998 tournament. They were guided by their inspirational **talisman** Zinedine Zidane.

Midfield maestro

Zidane gave footballing masterclasses on the field. He could do everything well – pass, control, dribble, head, shoot. And Zidane looked so elegant while he played that he was described as football's answer to the ballet.

Zidane's ball control made him one of the greatest midfielders of all time.

National hero

Zidane became an instant national hero in 1998. The French hosts faced defending champions and favourites Brazil in the World Cup final. Man of the Match Zidane scored two headers from corners as France cruised to a 3-0 victory.

Two years later France were crowned European Championship winners. This time Zidane was voted Player of the Tournament. The winning moment in the final was a dramatic golden goal by striker David Trezeguet.

Galactico

In the early 2000s, Real Madrid were on a mission to sign the world's biggest superstars (*galacticos*). This included Portuguese winger Luís Figo and Englishman David Beckham. But Zidane was the most expensive signing of them all, joining from Juventus for a then world record €78 million. Zidane's match-winning volley for Madrid in the 2002 Champions League final is often called the greatest goal in the competition's history. In 2003, Zidane was named World Player of the Year for the third time.

Around the world

FIFA were keen for World Cups to be played in all corners of the globe. In 2002, Japan and South Korea hosted the first tournament in Asia. The tournament was full of surprises. Champions France were knocked out in the group stage and South Korea reached the semi-finals. Brazil won a record fifth title, beating Germany 2-0 in the final.

TALES FROM HISTORY

At Euro 2004 nobody gave Greece a chance. In fact Greece had never even won a game at a major tournament. However, they did the unthinkable. The key to their success was sturdy defending. From the quarter-final onwards they won every match 1-0, beating champions France and the Czech Republic, and then hosts Portugal in the final.

Exit Zidane

France reached the World Cup final again in 2006 to face Italy. Zidane, who had announced that the final would be the last game of his career, gave France an early lead from the penalty spot, but Marco Materazzi soon levelled.

Then, in extra time, Zidane had a moment of madness. Upset at something, Zidane turned around and headbutted Materazzi in the chest! Zidane was sent off and his career was over. Without their best penalty taker, France were defeated in the shoot-out. Despite his red card, Zidane was awarded the Golden Ball.

Greece's Angelos Charisteas heads the winning goal against France at Euro 2004.

SPANISH DOMINANCE

Since the mid-2000s, Spanish teams have dominated European and club competitions. And between 2008 and 2012, Spain became the first nation to win three major tournaments in a row.

Xavi the heartbeat

In 2008, Spain won their first European Championship since 1964. Fernando Torres scored the only goal of the final against Germany. Player of the Tournament Xavi was the heartbeat of the Spanish side. In central midfield he controlled the flow of the game with his incredibly accurate passing.

Xavi (left) rarely gave the ball away.

Tiki-taka

Spain weren't big and tough, so they had to outpass their opposition. Xavi and other small players, such as Andrés Iniesta, dizzied their opponents with their short passing and movement. Their style of football became known as *tiki-taka*.

Spain's 2010 World Cup winning side were one of the best in the tournament's history. No one had an answer to *tiki-taka* and Spain claimed their first world title with a 1-0 win over the Netherlands in the final. Iniesta scored the winning goal in extra time with four minutes left on the clock. In 2012, Spain destroyed Italy 4-0 in the European Championship final and became the first team to win two Euros in a row.

Spain won their third major tournament in a row at Euro 2012.

FLASH FACT

Between 2006 and 2009, Spain equalled a Brazilian record of 35 matches unbeaten before they suffered a surprise 2-0 defeat to the United States.

Argentina's Lionel Messi has helped Barcelona become one of the best sides in the world.

TALES FROM HISTORY

Spain's terrific run ended quickly at the 2014 World Cup. They crashed out after just two games in the group stage. Brazil suffered an even greater humiliation. In the semi-final, their collapse against Germany was the worst ever defeat by a host nation.

By half-time Germany were 5-0 up and had scored four goals in the space of just six minutes! Brazil finally scored in the last minute, but by then they were losing 7-0! Miroslav Klose's strike for Germany saw him become the all-time leading World Cup goalscorer with 16 goals. Germany went on to win the World Cup for a fourth time.

Spanish clubs

Barcelona and Real Madrid are Spain's two greatest clubs and between them they have won seven out of the last 11 Champions Leagues. Real Madrid won three in a row between 2016 and 2018 and now have a record 13 European Cup victories. Spanish club Sevilla have also been dominant in Europe, winning a record five UEFA Cups/ **Europa Leagues** since 2006.

Portugal vs France

Since 2016, Portugal and France have shared out the top honours. At Euro 2016, Cristiano Ronaldo captained his nation to their first ever triumph in a major tournament, beating hosts France 1-0 in the final in extra time. Two years later France responded by winning the World Cup. Wonderkid and star of the future Kylian Mbappé scored in the 4-2 defeat of Croatia in the final.

Every Ballon d'Or award between 2008 and 2017 was won by either Cristiano Ronaldo (right) or Lionel Messi. Both players share the record of winning it five times.

GLOSSARY

Europa League an annual competition for European clubs that have performed well in their national leagues and cups. Before 2010, the competition was called the UEFA Cup.

extra time thirty added minutes when the score is tied after ninety minutes

FIFA the international governing body of football. FIFA stands for Fédération Internationale de Football Association.

formation the arrangement of a team's players on the pitch during a game

foul an action which breaks the rules of the game, such as tripping, pushing or a handball

free kick a kick of the ball awarded to a side because of a foul by the opposition

goal kick a free kick taken inside a team's own penalty box after the attackers have knocked the ball over the goal line to the sides of the goal

Golden Ball an award given to the best player at the World Cup

Golden Boot an award given to the top scorer in a competition

hat-trick the scoring of three goals in one game by one player

host the country that holds a major footballing event

innovations new ideas or methods

international a football fixture between two nations

knockout a tournament in which the losers at each stage are eliminated

legs the matches played between two clubs that decide which team advances to the next stage of a competition

Magyars a name given to people who speak Hungarian and are associated with the nation of Hungary

medieval relating to a period of history between the years c.500 and 1500 CE

munitions military weapons and equipment

offside a position on the field where a player cannot be passed the ball. To be onside, players must have two opponents between themselves and the opponent's goal.

penalty a free shot from the penalty spot (11 metres from goal) with just the goalkeeper to beat

penalty shoot-out a contest where each side takes at least five penalties to decide the outcome of a match

prolific producing many goals

public school a secondary school where pupils are charged fees to attend

Soviet Union a huge country that split into 15 independent nations in 1991, including Russia

substitute a player who replaces a teammate during a game

talisman an influential player who is thought to bring good fortune

top-flight the highest division in a nation's league structure

volley a strike of the ball made before it touches the ground

West Germany a former country that reunited with East Germany in 1990 to form present-day Germany

Yugoslavia a former nation in south-east Europe that since 1992 has broken into seven independent countries, including Croatia and Serbia

FURTHER INFORMATION

BOOKS

An Infographic Guide to: Football,
Wayland, 2016

Soccer Record Breakers,
Clive Gifford, Carlton Books, 2017

The Football Encyclopedia,
Clive Gifford, Kingfisher, 2016

The Story of Football,
Grant Bage, Collins, 2016

WEBSITES

www.myfootballfacts.com
This site contains a mountain of stats, including past cup champions and top goalscorers.

www.uefa.com
History and stats can be found here for every UEFA European competition.

www.fifa.com/news/classic-football.html
Tales from history on the FIFA website including classic matches and legends of the game.

www.bbc.co.uk/timelines/zp2mmp3
The story of the FIFA World Cup.

www.footballsgreatest.weebly.com/legends.html
Football's greatest legends.

INDEX